UNCOMMON CAREER
SUCCESS

UNCOMMON CAREER
SUCCESS

Straight Talk From
America's Premier Executive Coach

VANCE CAESAR, Ph.D.

Seal Beach, California

Published by PCH Publishing
3020 Old Ranch Parkway, Third Floor
Seal Beach, CA 90740

Publisher's Cataloguing-in-Publication Data
Caesar, Vance

    Uncommon career success : straight talk from American's
    premier executive coach / Vance Caesar. –1st ed. –Seal Beach,
    CA : PCH Publishing, 2003.

    p. ; cm.
    ISBN: 0-9670855-1-9

    1. Success in business. 2. Success. I. Title.

HF5386 .C34 2004   2003115317
650.1–dc22   0402

Book coordination by Jenkins Group, Inc. • www.bookpublishing.com
Cover design by Kelli Leader
Interior design by Debbie Sidman/Paw Print Media

Printed in the United States of America
07 06 05 04 03 • 5 4 3 2 1

For Mother Teresa and her teachings of love, focus, and power toward serving God and ourselves by serving others.

Acknowledgments

Thanks to my wife of 36 years, Carol Ann Caesar, Ph.D., for her insights into psychology and her constant support as we have journeyed together along a path of learning and loving each other, our family, and our clients. Thank you, too, for your tireless editing of this manuscript.

Special recognition goes to the Franklin-Covey organization for publishing many of my writings about priorities in our lives and how these determine who we are.

Kudos to Brooke Bischoff, Colleen Romero, and Linda Kau, who shepherded this and so many other projects to fruition. You have my respect and admiration for who you are becoming each day.

Contents

Introduction

Often, when we get to the finish line called success, we simply don't feel successful enough. We feel an emptiness as we work harder, achieve more, and do all the things we should do to succeed. This is common—and sad. It's the path to burnout, frustration, and sometimes resentment. This book is about achieving uncommon career success—having a career that creates the life you want.

Yes, we have an option: UNCOMMON CAREER SUCCESS!

Be successful—feel successful—and get energized by your work.

Eight specially selected chapters show you the way. Each is a short ride to greater career success and uncommon levels of joy and pride in yourself and your work. At the end of each chapter is a section titled Personal Coach with suggestions for personal action as you coach yourself to true, uncommon career success.

CHAPTER 1

Seven Steps to a Joy-Filled Career

A joy-filled career? Yes, you can have more than an OK career. Today's job market offers you a unique chance to create a joy-filled career. Here's how to take advantage of a possible once-in-a-lifetime opportunity.

I have observed highly successful managers and executives who say they have found joy—a lot of joy—in their careers. Here's what they have in common:

1. A life purpose they can articulate
2. Life goals they always keep in mind
3. Meaningful work
4. Association with energy-giving people

5. Beliefs that create joy at work
6. Three Rs: Review, Renew, and Recommit
7. Discipline

1. A Life Purpose They Can Articulate

Successful and joy-full managers, executives, entrepreneurs, and leaders have often written their life purpose as a personal mission statement. Usually they have been able to summarize their life purpose with one word, called their Word-in-the-Box.

When I was president of a division of Knight Ridder Newspapers in Southern California, my Word-in-the-Box was Leadership. I strove every day to offer appropriate, responsive, and responsible leadership to all my constituencies. Comparing my daily activities to my Word-in-the-Box forced me to ask myself every day, "Am I offering the right kind of leadership today? Am I living my purpose? Am I walking my talk?"

As I became an owner of community newspapers, my Word-in-the-Box changed to Service. After all, small weekly newspapers are more about service than leadership or anything else.

As an executive coach since 1992, my Word-in-the-Box is now Responsibility. My life purpose is to guide people toward forming a more responsible world, one client at a time. It is also to help each client develop more response-ability, that is, to have more tools to fruitfully respond to what happens to them.

What is your Word-in-the-Box?
Knowing it will help you focus on your life purpose.
It will also help you decide what not to do, which is also
a key to being joy-full.
My Word–in-the-Box is:

---

2. Life Goals They Always Keep in Mind

My life goals stem from answers to four key questions.
Ask yourself these questions and consider thoughtful
answers.

- **What do I want to feel?**

Love, loved, proud, successful, significant. Choose
concepts that have emotional impact for you.

- **What do I want to do?**

Have a family. Climb Mt. Kilimanjaro. Bowl 300.
Scuba. Go to school. Listen to yourself and write down
things that feel important for you to do.

- **What do I want to own?**

A million-dollar house or bank account. How about a
racing yacht, a thriving business, a reputation as the top
sales manager in your industry, or a great reputation?

Use your imagination to tap into the possibilities that truly reflect your real desires.

■ **What do I want to contribute?**

Peace to those whose lives you touch, a thriving neighborhood, a successful family, love. What might be a legacy?

I have answers to these four questions for this year as well as for age 90. This year's answers are on a three-by-five card on our refrigerator door. My goals are posted next to my wife's. We update our life goals (and create new three-by-five cards) each year during our full day of life planning between Christmas and New Year's Day. This practice has added harmony and clarity to our 36 years of marriage.

Your life goals may be expressed in a different form. You might draw a picture depicting your goals for this year. You could write a story or poem in which you describe your goals and what your life will be like when you achieve them. You could even record an audiotape of your goals; then play the tape in your car every Monday on your way to work.

Prioritize your wants so you can achieve—or make great progress toward achieving—some of them during the next 12 months. Keep in mind the importance of your personal life, which includes relationships with God, family, friends, and associates, your physical health and fitness, and a financial plan with targets for net worth and annual income. This will help keep your life plan in focus as you create and achieve your career plan.

After you have adjusted your plans and goals to eliminate conflicts—such as goals requiring greater resources of fitness or finances than you have obtained—your tripod of plans (personal, financial, and career) will work together to create the life you really want.

Notice an important concept in the four life-planning questions. Nowhere do they ask what you should do. Instead they all ask what you want to do with your life. The difference between doing what we really want to do and what we feel we should, ought, or need to do—often to satisfy conventions pressure-pumped into our lives—may be enormous.

You probably won't achieve all of your life goals next year. In fact, if you can, you may have aimed too low. In this case you may want to consider boosting some aspirations to challenge you to perform at a higher level.

The point is not how you do it, but to do it. Give yourself the many gifts of having specific goals. Life goals will help you stay focused on what's important. The following four books are wonderful resources to assist you in creating the focus that will add joy to your career and your life:

FIRST THINGS FIRST: to Live, to Love, to Learn, to Leave a Legacy, Stephen R. Covey, 1994. This best seller is an excellent aid in writing life goals.
I COULD DO ANYTHING IF I ONLY KNEW WHAT IT WAS: How to Discover What You Really Want and How to Get It, Barbara Sher and Barbara

Smith, 1994. Many creative and helpful exercises to jumpstart your discovery process.

LEADERSHIP FROM THE INSIDE OUT, Kevin Cashman, 1998. This is the cornerstone book I use in the doctoral level Self-Leadership course I teach at Pepperdine University.

THE ART OF POSSIBILITY: Transforming Professional and Personal Life, Rosamund Stone Zander and Benjamin Zander, 2000. Written by an amazing couple, this easy-to-read book reminds us of the fundamental possibilities in front of us every day.

3. Meaningful Work

Doing meaningful work that daily moves you closer to achieving your life goals is the third step toward creating a joy-filled career. When each day's work is aligned with your life purpose, the day has more meaning and joy.

What determines whether the work is meaningful? Often it's not the work itself. How you experience the work is what defines its meaningfulness. The following story of the three bricklayers poignantly demonstrates this insight.

Three workers were asked, "What are you doing?"

The first bricklayer said, "I'm making a dollar for every six bricks I lay. I hate this job, but I have to pay the rent. So here I am."

The second one said, "I'm about to finish this wall that will support the roof. But what I'm really doing is thinking about when my wife and I can really start living." "When will that be?" he was asked. "We'll start really living when I retire. That's when we'll travel all around the country in our dream motor home, just like that one gliding down the highway right now," he indicated with an envious expression. Brushing his envy aside, he went on excitedly, "Just think, it's only seven years, three months, one week, and two days until my wife and I can really start living."

The third bricklayer said, "I'm improving lives—and what I do will keep on improving lives for decades after I die. Can you see what we're constructing here? It's a place of worship where people will find God and the peace offered to them. They'll take that feeling home, into their workplace and their neighborhoods, and the world will be better by what I do today. And when I retire, I'll volunteer for Habitat for Humanity so I can continue to lay bricks and make a difference in people's lives."

The third bricklayer has created meaningful work that daily gets him closer to achieving his life goals, and is aligned with his life purpose. What joy!

My father is 83. He plays golf four times a week. What's meaningful about that? For him, playing golf well is an art and an expression of respect for a game that has countless life lessons in every round. Yes, he loves to win tournaments. But, there's much more to it. The game's meaningfulness radiates from him every time he loosens up for another round of lessons, especially those shared with his grandchildren. He, too, has found meaningfulness in his labor, and alignment with his purpose. And you should see the joy shine on his face as he almost dances along each golf hole!

Whether it's laying bricks or playing golf, you too can create meaning in your work every day. As you do, you have taken the third step toward creating a joy-filled career.

4. Association with Energy-Giving People

Some people at work take energy from you, while others give you energy. Often it's entirely up to you to choose with whom you share your career. Often you can freely choose between those who take and those who give you energy. However, circumstances may appear to limit your freedom to choose, which means taking this important step will require persistence and diplomacy. Give this endeavor what it takes, because protecting and enhancing your energy is vital to achieving a joy-filled career.

One way to think about this is to list all the people with whom you will, or could, spend time during the next two weeks. Then go over the list with two high-lighters, one green, one red. Highlight in green the names of people who give you energy when you're with them. Highlight in red those who take energy when you are with them.

Create a plan, perhaps with help from a career coach, to maximize your time with the greens. Also, develop a plan to limit the time spent with the reds. Review your progress with your coach every 90 days or so.

5. Beliefs That Create Joy at Work

Our beliefs have a lot of power in determining how we feel and how we act towards others. The more hopeful, positive, and optimistic our belief system that we take to work each day is, the greater the probability that we will be energized and joy-full.

Examine your beliefs about your work. Write them down and ask yourself, "How accurate are these beliefs?" and "What can I do to accentuate the energizing ones and decrease or fix the de-energizing ones. Create reminders, perhaps on your calendar, desk, or laptop, that allow you to regularly visit the energizing beliefs.

Your church, synagogue, mosque, or temple may already give you energy every day. If not, be good enough to yourself to be involved in a practice that gives you frequent doses of energy each day on the job. Some people have developed ways to meditate and exercise which have proven helpful for them.

6. Three Rs: Review, Renew, and Recommit

Constantly review what's working and what's not working. Renew what's working or what could work. Then recommit (don't re-dabble) to your renewed purpose, goals, and relationships as you complete the cycle.

How might YOU review, renew, and recommit? Try a personal retreat of two hours each month where you consider where you are in your life and what you are actually doing and compare this to your purpose and goals. Consider the possible alterations that would fine-tune your choices for the next month. Write these down. Then review them, renew your inspiration, and recommit to the discipline of carrying out the top two or three choices.

Review, renew, and recommit to the life, work, relationships, and beliefs you really want.

7. Discipline

Here's the catch! It takes discipline to get into and stay in this joy-full condition. Often, discipline is enhanced by having a coach help us hold ourselves accountable (see page 18). Sometimes it's from your accountability group (see pages 31–32), your journal writing, or even your children. Whatever forms you select, commit to maintain the level of discipline you know will support a joy-filled career.

Personal Coach

1. Use your Word-in-the-Box to guide writing your life purpose. Add a second word, then a third. With three core words you're really on your way to adding three more. Keep adding one word at a time until you can string them together into a purpose statement, with help from connector words such as and, by, and toward.

2. Using the knowledge gained from defining your life purpose and answering the four questions (pages 3–4), write your life goals that are in alignment with your life purpose.

3. Select your goals for the next year. Post them where you see them daily.

4. Consider your work and think of ways to find meaningfulness in it, just like the third brick-layer. Write these down. Review them weekly, at least.

5. Decide on ways you will surround yourself with people who give you energy. Follow through on at least one of these every month.

6. Find and practice a belief system and specific behaviors that daily lighten your work life. Examples could be: affirmations, prayer, spiritual

readings, yoga, singing, listening to uplifting music, walking, adding to your gratitude list, sharing with a spiritual mentor, etc.

7. Create a plan for reviewing, renewing, and recommitting to your purpose, your goals, and the meaningfulness in your work.

8. Commit to what it takes for you to have the discipline to do the above.

CHAPTER 2

You, Inc.: Minding Your Own Business

Top entrepreneurs manage their businesses with at least nine keys to achievement. Here's how you can win greater success and personal fulfillment by putting these to work managing your career as if _you_ were a business.

Want to increase your income, enhance your career, feel more fulfilled? Two decades of studying "Winning Edge" entrepreneurs (those in the top three percent of their industry or profession) have turned up nine keys to help accomplish these goals.

Nine keys used by winning entrepreneurs:

1. Have a written business/career plan that is in harmony with your life purpose.
2. Satisfy an unmet need better than anyone else.
3. Understand (and really know) your customers better than your competitors.
4. Anticipate your customers' needs better than your competitors.
5. Invest in your future.
6. Be passionate about your business/career and your role in it.
7. Recruit a championship coaching staff.
8. Develop a well-honed exit strategy.
9. Remember that everything counts.

1. Have a Written Business/Career Plan

According to numerous studies of successful and failed businesses, having a written business plan (including financial projections) that is contributed to by a championship coaching staff is the most important criterion in predicting a venture's success.

Entrepreneurs who are successful often invest time in writing their game plans and goals. They also plan how they are going to achieve each goal. They often have a well-versed chief financial officer or financial coach to ensure that they stay on top of their cash flow, their profit after taxes, and their balance sheet.

Keep your written plans and goals where you can review your progress at least monthly. Update your plan, including your net worth, at the same time each year. Your coach can help you fine tune your plan and help keep you focused on uncommon career success.

2. Satisfy an Unmet Need

Winners think empathetically, not egotistically. They focus on being best at satisfying the needs of others, not on what they want to sell to others. The former is a service or giving mentality. The latter is a selfish or getting mentality.

Examples of the service mentality include Walt Disney, who wanted to give the world's families at least a few hours of happiness when he opened Disneyland almost fifty years ago. The Nordstrom family wanted to give superior service to their shoppers. Jeep wanted to give a feeling of adventure and independence to Jeep owners. Each thought in terms of the customers' needs they could best satisfy.

Think and talk empathetically. Describe your work in terms of what needs of others you satisfy. Doing the same thing in your resumé is far more effective than merely listing your experience or your responsibilities.

3. Understand Your Customers

The uncommonly successful have honed their empathetic skills and have learned to understand their customers' needs, values and decision-making styles better
than their competitors. Most of those with whom I have
worked have gotten to know each core customer so well
that they can speak in terms the customer finds easy to
understand and act upon.

The uncommonly successful often use behavioral and
communications tools to help them understand their customers better. Among the commonly used tools are the
concepts in the Meyers-Briggs Type Indicator (MBTI).

These concepts, written about in numerous books,
help one understand how others prefer to take in information and how they prefer to make decisions.
Knowing this can give you a huge competitive advantage in meeting their needs.

Personality inventories and behavioral tools can
strengthen your understanding of yourself and others
as you learn how people prefer to behave and why.
Become knowledgeable about these vital tools. When
you do, your communications will be much more effective. You'll accomplish more with less effort.

4. Anticipate Your Customers' Needs

Wayne Gretzky once told me his secret to scoring 2,500
points faster than anyone else in the National Hockey

League: "I skate to where the puck is going to be better than most players. This gives me a huge advantage." Bill Gates would probably say something similar. These winners demonstrate a special ability to anticipate where the need is going to be. And they get there first, prepared to maximize their advantage.

Is this some mysterious gift other people were born with, but you weren't? Not at all. As with most skills, anticipation is learned. The first step is to get into the habit of consistently thinking about anticipating your customers' needs.

To give yourself the ability to anticipate needs better than your competitors, invest time in developing anticipatory skills and knowledge. To reach—and stay on—the cutting edge of change, listen to tapes by futurists like Faith Popcorn. Also, attend lectures by leading-edge thinkers at your local college, or join a mastermind group of people who think out of the box.

5. Invest in Your Future

Successful careerists invest part of their income in future growth and increased value. Some of the items invested in are: (a) learning more about customers, (b) advancing their technology and knowledge of it, (c) strengthening their team, and (d) preparing themselves for the future— physically, emotionally, and spiritually. Their spending plan supports their written developmental plan. Remember, take-home pay isn't yours until there is an investment that further increases your value.

6. Be Passionate

Uncommonly successful careerists are some of the most passionate people with whom I have had the privilege of working. They are like the third bricklayer discussed in Chapter One. They find their gift, and they pass it on to make the greatest difference in the world that they can. They know the word passion is really three words:

Pass - I - On

And they do that each day!

Manage your career with the third bricklayer's perspective. Find the higher purpose in what you do, or do something else. Finding passion in everyday activities is one of the most valuable gifts you can give yourself.

An optimized career is filled with Pass - I - On. Many leaders who have optimized careers say the key to their success is discovering and developing their natural gifts and spending the rest of their lives passing these on to others. David Nordstrom, Oprah Winfrey, Jimmy Carter, and Billy Graham describe how they became successful by passing on their gifts. They show us that living life passionately gives us energy and attracts others to us.

7. Recruit a Championship Coaching Staff

Tiger Woods is great, partly because he has great coaches. To optimize your career, get yourself a great career coach.

If possible, choose a coach who has earned the right to coach you to where you want to go. This will be someone who has values you respect, and who has already delivered to others the coaching results you want. Ask people who have coaches for referrals. Contact organizations mentioned throughout this book for more information on how to select a coach that will best fit your needs and your budget.

One of the many aspects of having a top career coach is that he or she will help you find your optimum levels and types of stress. They will suggest ways for you to consider: (1) replacing negative stressors with positive stressors, and (2) using stress to your advantage. They will also help you generate feedback that fuels your fun and your learning.

Champions who optimize their golf games, their entrepreneurial success, and their careers have coaches. You deserve one, too.

Sometimes, people have different coaches who have different areas of expertise. My entrepreneurial coaching staff has included the coaches already mentioned, plus a spiritual coach and a marriage coach. They have changed over the years, as they and I have changed. Uncommonly successful people have frequently told me about the great value their coaching staffs have added to their lives and to the success of their ventures.

You can create a coaching staff that is tailored to your interests. The uncommonly successful careerist's coaching staff includes experts with complementary skills who are committed to their success. Sometimes your coaching staff will meet as a group with you. Or they may never know each other.

8. Develop a Well-Honed Exit Strategy

Knowing where he or she wants to end up helps the uncommonly successful careerist choose the best team and the best path for the journey. Whether the goal is going public or selling to a competitor or vendor, the entrepreneur's clear exit strategy helps her or him make better decisions more quickly and easily.

- First, define your career destination in your mind.
- Second, set it down in writing.
- Third, set a date by which you will have accomplished your exit and moved on to the next goal.

This is *the big picture*. Getting it clearly established will help you keep short-term challenges in perspective. Big picture awareness also helps your written career plan get you where you want to end up.

9. Remember That Everything Counts

This idea is repeated throughout this book to emphasize the point. Everything either helps or hinders the progress of the uncommonly successful careerist. Your friends. The clothes you wear. What you read. The exercise you get. Even what and where you eat. So does the TV you watch, the clubs and the organizations you join, and the hobbies and activities you pursue. Everything counts.

Use all of your resources and activities to achieve your goals. Recognize that everything you do each day plays a role in your career and your life. Make sure that everything you do moves you toward—rather than away from—meeting each of your goals.

You can use entrepreneurial skills to build your competence and success. The nine keys help to mind your career as if it were your business. Because it is.

Personal Coach

1. Keep in mind the question, "What is the perceived unmet need of my company, my industry, my customers?" Write down ideas and consider which ones on which to act.

2. Discover opportunities for improving your communications and listening skills. Act on one.

3. As you consider your career goals, identify an area in which you want to enhance your skills. Look in your community, on the Internet, in professional journals, and ask others so you can discover your best opportunities for growth.

4. At the beginning of each day, ask and answer the question, "What will I be passionate about today?"

5. Consider how you'll go about creating a championship coaching staff for yourself. First, list what kinds of coaches are most important to you now. Second, discover and list the individuals who could meet each of your needs. Third, interview candidates to determine who will be the best match for your needs and circumstances.

6. All good things must end! How long do you want to stay where you are? Set a date. Know where you will go next.

7. Plan how you'll keep this concept constantly in mind: Everything counts!

8. Spend no more than fifteen minutes today—why not right now?—writing out the best five-year business/career plan for yourself you can think of right now with annual benchmarks that include title, responsibility, authority, income, and planned learning which invests in your future.

   Having worked through the seven items above may give you ideas, information, and added inspiration. So set your inhibitions aside and just get it done. You can revise it later. It's a start on this essential step to lifting your career to new heights.

   Again, spend no more than fifteen minutes on this first draft of putting your plan in writing.

9. Confirm that your career plan is aligned with your written life plan, including similar benchmarks such as goals for family, church, community, and net worth.

CHAPTER 3

Lifeboards for Your Career—and Life

Do as Ken does. Use a lifeboard to launch you to success in your career and in your private life.

As always, Ken's board meeting began at 7:30 a.m. sharp. All six of his lifeboard members were ready for Ken's progress report. They knew their time to respond would come shortly.

When Ken finished reporting on his career progress for the last six months and his plans for the next six months, breakfast would be ordered. Then Ken's lifeboard members would go to work responding to his report with accolades, questions, offers, and sometimes challenges.

Ken had assembled his mostly volunteer lifeboard of advisors for their semiannual 90-minute meeting over breakfast at the round table in the back of Ken's favorite restaurant. The agenda included an update on Ken's career and how it was supporting his life goals. He also updated them on his financial progress and his personal progress related to the five-year plan he had presented to them two years previously. The accountability and the support they had given him during the past 24 months had paid huge dividends.

Ken is one of my clients. He tells me he feels substantially happier and more productive since creating his own board. "I feel I have been launched to a new level of results and rewards," he says.

Why did Ken form his lifeboard? He noticed that boards of directors and less formal boards of advisors helped other high achievers in their lives. CEOs, executive directors, and professional athletes seemed to have groups of advisors helping them get more out of their work and their lives.

Ken knew many successful entrepreneurs and executives belonged to groups like The Executive Committee (TEC), Young Presidents Organization (YPO), Renaissance Executive Forum (REF), and Young Leaders Organization (YLO). (See Resource Information, page 31–32). Others had accountability and support groups from their church, synagogue, or community.

Ken also looked at his friend Tom's experience. Tom had family meetings involving two or three generations of experienced, caring relatives to help him stay focused on getting the most out of his career and his life. The common ingredient of every effective lifeboard is caring, committed, and competent people who focus on a person's success.

It's easy to see the benefits of having your own lifeboard of advisors: focus, accountability, and resources accelerate your results while reducing your effort. Sharing your written developmental plan with your lifeboard allows them to hold you accountable for your achievement of it. They can also help as you update the entire plan annually.

It can be challenging to communicate what you want in your career and your life and to be willing to share your plans and progress with others who have much more experience and expertise than you possess at this stage of your career. This means revealing your strikeouts as well as your home runs. This can be somewhat intimidating at times. However, the program's great power to speed up your success comes from your willingness to make yourself accountable to your board.

If you are ready to step up to higher performance, get started by creating your lifeboard of advisors today. Another option is to join an existing accountability and support group. First, we will explore how you can create your own lifeboard.

1. What You'll Need

- The maturity to ask for someone's mentoring and coaching

- The willingness to have a written career plan that is aligned with your written life plan, perhaps enlisting a personal career coach to help you write your career plan
- The confidence to tell the truth about your successes and failures
- The courage to risk rejection by asking top people in your life to be part of your lifeboard
- Enough planning to organize a 90-minute review of your progress and plans, leaving at least two-thirds of the time for you to listen and log your board's responses and offers of assistance
- Enough openness to take your board's suggestions and offers seriously, including letting them know how you've used them, and with what results
- The knowledge that the members of your board enjoy helping you achieve your goals and probably often say that they get at least as much out of your board meetings as you do
- Enough assertiveness to exclude anyone who does not contribute adequately to your results
- The willingness to pick up the tab for everyone (from breakfast at approximately $50 per meeting to as much as $10,000 per year for monthly full-day meetings run by a professional facilitator)
- The organization to keep each member up-to-date as significant events occur between meetings

2. Members Your Lifeboard Will Need

Members who:

- are as caring and competent as they are aligned with your values and goals
- hold you accountable for doing what you say are the most important things for you to do toward achieving your career and your life goals, while respecting your right to progress as rapidly or as slowly as you choose
- have complementary skills and life experiences
- are skilled in empathizing and listening
- benefit from being with each other
- are knowledgeable about your business or your industry and are well connected with powerful people in the industry
- can maintain the confidentiality of each meeting
- gain something from being on your lifeboard

Here are examples of comments heard about being on Ken's board: "Helping Ken is fun." "Being on Ken's board this year got me well connected with somebody I probably wouldn't have met otherwise. It's helped my business a lot." "This is an opportunity for me to give something back after all the help I've received." "I think I'll develop my own lifeboard, too."

3. Finding Great Lifeboard Members

Consider school friends, chamber of commerce leaders, service club leaders, religious leaders, and even your insurance agent, attorney, CPA, banker, ex-professor, or stockbroker. Family members who have "been there, done that" are often glad to help.

People who have their own lifeboards, who now know the value of receiving mentoring and coaching, are often great at mentoring others.

Ask your local volunteer center and the Service Corps of Retired Executives (SCORE) plus other well-established nonprofit mentoring and coaching organizations dedicated to passing on counsel and resources.

The Professional Coaches and Mentors Association (PCMA), the International Coaches Federation (ICF), and other groups of mentors and coaches can suggest professionals who are often highly trained and experienced in helping create a lifeboard, or serving on it.

4. You Don't Have to Create Your Own Board

The key is to use the resources all around you to launch yourself to a higher level of performance and satisfaction with life. CEOs, entrepreneurs, and other high achievers rely on this to maintain their growth. You could join an existing group or other available accountability groups in your area.

Isn't it time you considered joining an existing lifeboard—or creating your own? I think it is.

Resource Information

SCORE

The Service Corps of Retired Executives is sponsored by the Small Business Administration. SCORE brings individuals and groups together in most communities in America, as they focus on their entrepreneurial goals and how these fit into their lives. (614) 469-2357

TEC WORLDWIDE

TEC, The Executive Committee, a worldwide organization, is based in San Diego, California. TEC helps CEOs, entrepreneurs, and key executives sharpen their focus and maintain alignment with their life goals by bringing together small groups of non-competing members to act as informal boards of advisors for one another. (800) 274-2367

YPO

The Young Presidents Organization is known as the nation's largest fraternity because it is made up of thousands of young company presidents. It also includes others in similar positions of responsibility.

They meet in their communities to help each other get more out of their careers and their companies. (800) 773-7976

REF

Renaissance Executive Forums is headquartered in La Jolla, California. REF brings business leaders and entrepreneurs together in small groups monthly to help them stay focused on their life priorities and their business goals. (858) 385-0502

PCMA

The Professional Coaches and Mentors Association is dedicated to lifelong learning. PCMA refers professional coaches and mentors to clients who, individually or in groups, want to stay focused on their career and their life goals. (949)679-4930 or pcmaonline.org

YLO

Young Leaders Organization is headquartered in Seal Beach, California. YLO is for proven leaders 25–39 years old who have personal and professional leadership interests and needs shared by those not yet at midlife. (562) 799-5560

Personal Coach

1. Make an exhaustive list of desirable lifeboard advisors, considering the plusses, minuses, and availability of each. Or join an existing lifeboard of advisors.

2. Contact the first six who you (and your coach if you have one) believe are best suited for your needs and theirs. Get commitments from as many of these as possible, contacting those on your list until you have six volunteers.

3. After recruiting a six-member lifeboard of advisors, set up a 90-minute meeting to review your career progress and plans. Set a timely date for your next lifeboard meeting.

4. Do your homework before the next meeting! Update your career goals and plans. Make sure your career goals support your life plan, which you will also update.

5. Join someone else's lifeboard as a mentor or coach.

CHAPTER 4

Manage Bosses

Want to optimize your career success? It's easy—or at least enormously easier—when you consider these ideas.

Study people who have great careers and you'll see them moving along, seemingly effortlessly. They have made a habit of getting everything their careers have to offer. Many of them utilize the following, which may be helpful to you.

1. Satisfy Your Boss's Needs

Peter Drucker, author of the classic business text *The Practice of Management* and one of the world's foremost management gurus, observes that the key to optimizing your career is to make your boss feel happy. This requires your being perceived as doing the right job with the right attitude, building the right relationships, and generally causing your boss to feel happy when he or she thinks of you.

Dr. Drucker is right. Make each boss a raving fan of yours by being perceived by your boss as the best at doing what you are paid to do. Plan how to make your boss feel happy tomorrow, the next day, and the next month by anticipating his or her needs better than other people with whom you are compared.

2. Serve the Right Bosses

Work for a boss you understand and who understands you. This is the easy way to produce results that make your boss feel happy. It's still possible to succeed even when there's no two-way feeling of understanding, although that means doing it the hard way.

Select bosses whose opportunities are expanding. For instance, deciding to work for senior banking executives at a time of massive bank consolidations would not be the easy way to create an optimum career.

Work for bosses who, as a group, are growing where you want to go, to where you see your career blossoming. If your optimum career involves international contacts, work for globally focused bosses like those in the airline industry. If you see success as staying in your hometown, maybe working for your town's school district or water board would serve you better.

3. Be Branded in the Minds of Target Bosses

If you don't stand for something, you stand for nothing. When you are known as the best sales manager, cost cutter, editorial writer, or software problem solver, you are substantially more attractive to bosses who need those results. You become at times an irresistible attraction.

Your branding as the best at something is the cornerstone. It is the "barrier to entry" you want to create by positioning your competitors as being second best in your bosses' minds. Volvo, which is branded as the safest vehicle, has positioned all other car manufacturers as second best in the area of automotive safety. In a similar fashion, you can position yourself so others are relegated to being known as second best.

How do you brand yourself as being the best? By being great first! Then, make sure the people who count are told about it. Do this in reverse order and you'll be known as the company's greatest blowhard.

4. Make Money

Making money is important to an optimized career. What is it you are being paid to do? Are you doing that? Are you meeting expectations set by you and your bosses for hitting your budget? For creating income?

In addition to these concerns, it is important to count profit after investing in some things like the following:

- Knowledge of your boss and his or her future needs
- Knowledge of your company's and your industry's technology
- Your reputation and your branding

PERSONAL COACH

1. Find out what is important to your boss and how you can be a part of creating that.

2. Describe (and write down) your ideal boss, considering what your career goals are.

3. Become known as the best at something. Identify what it is for which you want to be known as being the best. Identify how you can become the best at this. Then check with your boss/bosses to confirm how your reputation (or branding) compares to what you really want it to be.

4. What would be the best investment you could make to increase your knowledge of your company's needs and ways to meet one of them?

CHAPTER 5

Stakeholders: Your Guides to a Successful Career

Here's an easy way to leverage both stakeholders and the wisdom they hold.

Stakeholders have at least two things: a lot of interest in you and your career plus a lot of power over you and your career.

Who are your stakeholders?

Many of your friends probably have a lot of interest in your career success. If you have antagonists, they may have a lot of interest in your lack of success. Interest in your success or failure isn't enough, though, for any of these people to be a stakeholder.

Then there are those people with a lot of power over your career and where it could go, but they don't have a lot of interest in influencing it. Why? Because they just don't care enough about you to be one of your stakeholders. Examples include the senior executive who barely knows your name or the Human Resources VP who remembers your being hired, but hasn't really connected enough with you to champion your cause.

If people don't have a lot of interest in your success plus the power to influence it, they aren't your stakeholders.

Those who are uncommonly successful usually know who their stakeholders are—people who have an interest in and the power to influence their success or failure.

Stakeholder = Interest + Influence

A stakeholder can be a key customer, a core vendor, a critical lawmaker, or one of the executives in the company's game-maker/game-breaker positions. Successful entrepreneurs and those who think of their careers as their business consistently turn each key stakeholder into an advocate for their success.

Unusually successful careerists identify their top five to ten stakeholders every time they move into a new job or a new assignment. Make sure your top stakeholders are also your personal advocates. Focus on making your new stakeholders happy.

Don't make the mistake of diffusing your efforts by trying to be all things to all people, by trying to make everybody happy. Instead, focus your efforts on the few people who influence your success most—your handful of stakeholders.

Your first step is knowing who they are. This takes Emotional Intelligence (EI), as described in Daniel P. Goleman's three bestsellers. An important part of EI is empathy, which helps one to understand the needs of others, especially the most important "others," the people with a stake in your future.

After you've identified your top stakeholders, get to know each of them well enough to make sure you know exactly what their expectations are for you. How? One option is to ask them.

You could talk with each stakeholder about your desire to be successful. Ask what success would look like to her or him in six months. Get very clear on what each of your stakeholders really expects of you. Make your plans to address these. Then set up times to get their feedback. The frequency of feedback meetings often depends on the pace of change in the organization.

Or you could enlist an intermediary like a mentor or a coach. Often they can find out what you would need to do to be considered successful by each of the stakeholders (with whom you cannot directly communicate).

Once you are clear on what it's going to take to make each stakeholder a raving fan of yours, make sure you start doing it, or get another job immediately!

Constantly track how you are doing with each stakeholder. How? One way is to use the Stakeholder Relationships Scoreboard (SRS) on page 48. It's the best tool I know to track where you are with each stakeholder. Since communications usually precede relationships, this form may help you consider the status of your communications with those you desire to have or keep as stakeholders.

Plot where you've been, where you are, and where you are going with each of your stakeholder relationships. Review with your career mentor, coach, or trusted colleague what score you think you already have created with each stakeholder, what the score is today, and what it will take to ensure your score will be what you desire (in "flow") tomorrow.

"Flow" levels of communications feel as if you and the other person are communicating through a huge pipe with plenty of capacity, with no leakage and no obstacles to inhibit free and easy communications.

"Broke" levels of communications usually feel as if only part of the sender's message is being received. It's like passing a liquid message through a broken underground pipe with many holes in it; only some of what is sent gets there, and what is received is contaminated from dirt seeping into the line. Communications at this level seem closed, difficult, untrusting, critical, and ego-centered.

Take a few minutes now and pencil in on the Stakeholder Relationships Scoreboard where you are with three typical stakeholders: your boss, your boss's boss, and his or her assistant. On a scale of one to ten, rate your communications with each. Empathetic skills are helpful here as you consider how the other person perceives your rapport with them. If you are in the eight, nine or ten range, we call that score "flow." When your communications are in "flow," your relationships are usually open, free-flowing, trusting, supportive, and empathetic.

Trying to be in "flow" with everyone at work is almost impossible. I think that for most of us, it's unfair to even try to be in "flow" with everyone. It is also ineffective to try, as it weakens your focus on your stakeholders.

After you have assured yourself you are in "flow" with your top five to ten stakeholders, it could make sense to create a wider circle of "flow" relationships. You could add influential subordinates, key customers, longtime vendors, an influential peer, or even your board chair. But make sure as you go wider that you don't risk losing your core stakeholder support, which usually spells disaster.

Sometimes you will find you have "broke" communications with one or more of your top stakeholders. Elevating that stakeholder's "broke" communications to "OK" or "flow" is crucial to your success! I have seen dozens of senior executives lose great jobs by ignoring that simple truth.

You probably already know how to lift "broke" communications toward "flow." Why? You probably remember doing it elsewhere in your life. Maybe it was with your parents, your children, your spouse, your siblings, your teachers, or even one of your coaches. If so, that's a great place to mentally start—where you've been successful before.

How did you create "flow" communications? Probably by being empathetic, supportive, open, honest, and focused on creating win-win outcomes. These are all "flow" behaviors! You can't control your stakeholders' reactions to your behaviors. But you can control your own behaviors!

Here's an example. I was working with a CEO who discovered on the day of our coaching appointment that he had prostate cancer. He was scared. We talked about his controlling what he could control. Thirty minutes into our session, he said his 50th birthday was coming up in twelve days. I asked him, "If you could have anything for your birthday, what would it be?"

Tears came to his eyes.

"The best present I could possibly have would be to be reunited with my 28-year-old daughter," he said.

It seems three years earlier he had threatened to disown her if she married "that bum," which, of course, she did. "I haven't talked to her in over three years, and I miss her terribly," he said sadly.

I got up and told him I would return to his office in 20 minutes and ask him how the phone call went. He knew what phone call I meant.

Walking back into his office 20 minutes later, I felt the difference in this normally tough senior executive. Overjoyed, he almost cried out, "My daughter and I are having lunch together on my birthday!"

He had practiced "flow" behaviors. He was empathetic, supportive, open, and honest as he began the long road back to having his daughter be part of his life. He focused his behaviors on the outcome he really wanted with perhaps the most important stakeholder in his life at that time.

Here is what I know about "flow" communications with stakeholders:

We can't get to "flow" relationships with "broke" communications and behaviors. "Flow" relationships are healthy relationships. Like healthy bodies, they require an ongoing regime of stretching and working out to stay in shape.

Using a third party to help monitor and focus on maintaining "flow" communications usually helps immensely. Your scores on the Stakeholder Relationships Scoreboard are powerful predictors of your ability to attract resources and to create optimum career options.

A last note: optimizing future career choices includes focusing on your future stakeholders. They often are leaders in another part of your organization, influential people in your industry, or people who are highly respected in your profession. Top executive recruiters, influential editors, trade association presidents, and well-known mentors are also examples of potential stakeholders outside of your current stakeholder team.

Once you're consistently successful with your current stakeholders, consider focusing on the next set of stakeholders—they hold keys to your next career success.

Stakeholder Communications Scoreboard

		WAS	IS	WILL BE
	10			
Flow	9			
Fast/Easy	8			
	7			
	6			
OK	5			
	4			
	3			
Broke	2			
Stuck/Hard	1			

Flow (Green) Behaviors	Broke (Red) Behaviors
Attract	Avoid
Creative	Defensive
Effortless	Difficult
Plenty	Scarcity
Happy	Sad
Light	Heavy
Empathetic	Ego-centered

Stakeholders: Those special people in your career/business who have enough influence over *and* interest in determining your success (or failure).

Personal Coach

1. Identify your top five stakeholders in your current job. Create connections with your top five stakeholders, and make sure each of them knows your goals and your accomplishments.

2. Get clear about what each stakeholder expects from you.

3. Meet or exceed each expectation through focus, focus, focus.

4. Monitor how you are doing by routinely keeping score on the Stakeholder Communications Scoreboard (SCS).

5. Use a stakeholder mentor or coach to help your scoring on the SCS match your stakeholders' perceptions and to keep you focused.

6. Know who your top five stakeholders are outside your organization, and do the same things with them.

7. Based on your career plan, determine who the next five stakeholders will be. Plan how to best have them become interested in your success.

CHAPTER 6

Which Hurdle Is Tripping Your Career?

Bill, 38, needs to find a job. Why? Because he tripped and fell over one too many career hurdles last month. Bill didn't steal money or hit his boss. He's a good guy with a wife and two children who love him. His degree is from a respected university, and he's a good neighbor. He has it all—except a job.

Bill was one of those who were downsized last week. Why him and not the other guy? Because he fell where thousands before him have fallen—over one of the ten career hurdles that most frequently end a promising career. See if you can guess which one tripped him up one too many times.

Ten Career Hurdles

1. **Bill seemed arrogant, even rude at times.** Was it because he was in too much of a hurry to get the next thing done or because he had not fully developed his listening and empathy skills? Whatever it was, Bill's behavior didn't represent his intentions. It turned off too many subordinates and peers.

   He didn't use 360-degree feedback techniques to learn from those around him how his behaviors were being perceived, contributing to his career being derailed.

2. **Bill's ex-boss and ex-subordinates felt abandoned when he leapt into his current position.** "They felt you acted like a mercenary," Bill's boss told him a month before he was downsized. Too bad for Bill. He left a job and didn't leave friends who would sing his praises when they were queried by his new boss at the recent industry convention, where stories are shared so freely.

3. **Bill's attention span shortened, and his ability to concentrate waned as he became increasingly overloaded.** Key decisions were not getting the mental attention they deserved, and his relationships were becoming strained under the emotional weight. Thinking outside the box stops when even thinking inside the box becomes too great a

chore. Bill was noticeably less creative and less fun to be around.

4. **Bill began to look less healthy.** "I just don't have time to take care of my body right now. I'll get back in shape soon," he promised, as he continued to gain unwanted weight and eventually faced a panic-packed trip to the emergency room. It was a trip everyone in the office knew about 24 hours later, because a client's wife was in the ER the same night. Bill's boss wondered privately if the company could count on Bill as much as they had hoped.

5. **Bill's jargon scared the human resources director.** "I know he's kidding, but his words and gestures are exposing the company to a discrimination complaint or even a lawsuit," she told her boss, the VP of human resources, only three days before downsizing decisions were finalized.

6. **"I read in some court documents that Bill sued his previous employer over a disputed bonus payment,"** said the company's in-house counsel to the company's president the week before cutback decisions were made.

7. **"Guess what I heard from my husband,"** said the CEO's assistant. "Bill got his third traffic ticket in three months last week." That was 48 hours before Bill's position was consolidated with another one occupied by Bill's friend Jim, now the regional sales manager. Jim still wonders privately why he got the job instead of

Bill. "After all, Bill's numbers were always better than mine," Jim pointed out. "It's hard to figure."

8. **Bill's reliance on what had worked before blinded him to better ways of achieving his goals.** Becoming technologically competitive, like working out, was something he planned to do as soon as he could make the time. Meanwhile, he fell behind and was not looked upon as a rising star in the organization by key stakeholders and staff.

9. **Bill's career had been opportunistic at best.** He leaped into the latest job because it was so good he "couldn't afford to turn it down." Did it get him closer to where he wanted his career to be in twenty years? Did he even know where he wanted to be, and was he able to share his vision with his boss? No. Bill wondered why others seemed to be better understood and supported by their bosses.

10. **Bill's interests betrayed him,** especially his membership in African Trophies Unlimited. He wondered why the CEO's wife seemed against him. It never occurred to him that it started when she heard about the pictures of his latest hunting success that he had shown around the office. "Anyone who kills those beautiful creatures can't be trusted," she emotionally told anyone who would listen. Bill forgot that everything counts.

Which one of the ten career hurdles tripped Bill up one too many times? If you guessed number one you were right. If you guessed number ten you were right. Ditto with numbers two through nine. Each hurdle has tripped up scores of Bills I've met during the last thirty years. My research and that of others shows that most careers fail because of what the careerist didn't know he or she didn't know. Now you know what hurdles champions dance over—hurdles that others trip over. It's up to you now. It's your race to win.

Tips on Sailing over Career Hurdles

1. USE FEEDBACK AND CONSTANTLY IMPROVE YOURSELF.

Continuously invest in further strengthening your listening and empathy skills to better hear and understand the messages people are regularly sending. Taking classes and seminars, studying books, and getting 360-degree feedback can all help. Retaining a shadow coach, a coach who observes your interactions in many settings before recommending behavioral changes, is another tool champions employ. You can even videotape your performance. Yes, create a game video for study with your coach as you work constantly to improve your performance.

2. EXIT LIKE A CHAMPION.

Leave raving fans at each job when you depart. Know that the stories they tell will block or boost your career for years. Exit at least as well as you entered.

3. STAY SHARP.

Maximize your mental and emotional health. Plan breaks in your mental routine, during which you exercise your mind and emotions, like athletes exercise their bodies.

4. BE IN SHAPE.

Our bodies take us to the finish line. Having a champion's body makes it easier to finish first. A routine of adequate sleep each night, proper nourishment, and physical exercise all play a critical role in winning your career race. Consider hiring a personal trainer, and complete periodic comprehensive physicals as you run the race.

5. AUDIT YOUR ATTITUDES.

Ask a human resources expert to audit your behaviors and to explore your attitudes as they relate to you as a legal risk. For instance, growing up in some places may have produced behaviors or attitudes that could trip you up without your ever knowing it.

6. Resolve disputes privately.

Don't sue an employer unless it's your absolute last resort and you have carefully considered the career costs. Avoid this action even if you have obviously been wronged. Your track record follows you forever. Prospective employers will assume that if you initiated a lawsuit before, you're likely to do it again—against them. Having a good career coach often helps you avoid getting into such a dilemma, which creates a permanent public record of your inability to create win-win relationships.

7. Keep your record spotless.

Don't get arrested. Being arrested and being guilty are two different events in the courtroom and the boardroom. Whether it's for suspicion of DUI, disturbing the peace at your fraternity reunion, or a possible securities fraud, you have created a story that will haunt you forever.

8. Be a champion learner.

Avoid obsolescence both personally and professionally. It's not enough to be Internet literate while aiming at being the best manufacturing manager. Have state-of-the-art skills while you continue to learn new things to better prepare for tomorrow's jobs. Learn something new. From Aikido to zoning, there are exciting ways to learn new things.

9. STAY FOCUSED.

You know the importance of your company's having a finely honed strategic plan. In fact, you probably are pretty good at creating great plans for your department or your company.

Your career deserves—in fact demands—the same focus on the future. At least every two years, do a complete career strategic plan update. Use a S.W.O.T. (Strengths, Weaknesses, Opportunities, and Threats) analysis with the help of an experienced coach to focus on your career.

STRENGTHS	WEAKNESSES
1._____	1._____
2._____	2._____
OPPORTUNITIES	THREATS
1._____	1._____
2._____	2._____

10. ACT ON THIS FACT: EVERYTHING COUNTS.

Be aware that the role you play in the community, your hobbies, your spouse's behavior, what you read, eat, and watch on TV counts. Even the car you drive and the shoes you wear count. Make what you do in your life consistent with your career goals.

Personal Coach

---

1. Solicit feedback from subordinates, bosses, and peers. Check to see if others see you the way you perceive yourself. A 360-degree feedback instrument will show you specific strengths and areas on which to work. Your coach may help with this.

2. Evaluate yourself. Do you take your job for granted? Are you meeting the standards you did when you started your job, or have you become less concerned about important things like personal appearance? Spend a few minutes now to think about things you might be able to build on and to improve.

3. Utilizing information gathered from the above items, identify three things about yourself you want to improve. Make a plan right now to do something about one thing by the end of the week. For example, you may want to schedule a haircut, organize your time, get to important meetings on time, schedule lunch with a stakeholder, finish an overdue project, or listen better.

4. Discuss with your coach or mentor your plan for improvement.

CHAPTER 7

Career Freedom: Three Keys to Maximizing Your Options

The executive recruiter is on the other line. It's the third time this month you've had a call from someone wanting to offer you better work for a better boss. Maybe it's a dream, but maybe it's not.

For some people it is reality. They are the ones who constantly use the three keys to maximizing their career options. They have found a way to get more choices than 97 percent of others.

Three keys to maximizing your career choices and your worth in today's market are:

1. People Power

Maximize yourself by using influence, a support network, or connections.

2. Results

Maximize yourself by achieving results stakeholders can see.

3. Enhancing Your Skills

Maximize yourself by constantly developing and increasing your currently relevant skills.

Let's explore these further.

1. People Power

The first and most valuable key to maximizing yourself and your career options is often the least talked about: your people power. It's your ability to influence others to do what you want, while avoiding things you don't want done.

How do you get more people power? By being connected with others, so that you have an army of powerful people poised to help you get done what you want to get done any time, any place.

Let's explore how you can further develop your people power, since it is the most important key to maximizing your career success.

In 1980, when I was president of a Southern California daily newspaper, I met with the planners of the 1984 Olympics. I asked the top official why he was willing to dedicate the next five years of his life to a successful Olympics. "What in the world would make this project worth that much?" I asked.

He said, "When these Olympics are over, I will have created over 7,000 connections with people all over the world. My Rolodex will have increased in size at least tenfold."

"That's a lot of contacts," I replied.

"They're not contacts!" he said. Then he went on in a reverent whisper, "They are connections."

Connections, it turns out, are relationships with people for whom you have done something. Contacts are names of people you have met. There is a huge difference between connections and contacts.

"Here's the way I have it figured," he said. "Ninety percent of the people I do something for are aching to do something back for me. When the Olympics are over and I am trying to help someone, I'll have most of those 7,000 people aching to help me assist others. Can you imagine an army of almost 7,000, plus one, focused on making a colleague's life better? That's power," he said.

"Where did you learn the secret of getting power by giving?" I asked.

"I studied Mother Teresa's life," he said. "She can raise money faster than the most professional fundraisers I know," he said with great conviction.

If Peter Ueberroth were telling his story today, he'd probably point to Princess Diana's life as another example of how to gain this kind of power by giving—by connecting.

Red Scott, a 1984 recipient of the coveted Horatio Alger Award, told me that one thing common about his fellow awardees is their ability to connect with others by giving. "They are as ready to help others as any group I know," he said when talking with a group of Southern California senior executives. What allowed fellow Horatio Alger awardees like Billy Graham, Paul Harvey, Tom Landry, and Bob Hope to become so powerful? Their ability to convert contacts into connections.

That's it. The No. 1 key to maximizing your career choices and your value in our society is your ability to create connections with other influential people.

A year from now you could have increased your influence by 20 percent, 100 percent, or not at all. To get started, all you have to do is unselfishly, without expectation of repayment, help someone in your office, your company, or your profession.

The more people you help, the more connections you will likely create. The more connections you have, especially with other powerful people, the more people you'll have aching to help you help the next person and the next person. Before you know it, your power to produce results will mushroom. So, too, will your career choices. Sincerity is the secret. Remember not to expect payment or reward.

Congratulations! You've learned the secret of Mother Teresa and other people who have achieved extraordinary power.

2. Results

The second key is about results, that are enhanced by your ability to think and act empathetically. Think in terms of and talk about what others pay you to produce: results. Then get others to talk about the results you produce, especially stakeholders. Bear in mind that they are much more interested in your results than in your skills. It helps to understand what it is that they really want and what they view as positive results.

What matters is that the results you produce are clearly understood by those who count in your career. Your experience, the job titles you've held, and even the number of people who have reported to you are meaningless compared to the results you produce for those who invest in you. This is why on resumes we highlight accomplishments and quantify them. In business plans we stress the results the principals in the venture have produced, individually and collectively, which is what attracts investors.

Experienced business investors say they would rather bet on a mediocre technology implemented by a team that has repeatedly created success, than on a wonderful technology implemented by a team with no demonstrated results. They invest in results to get more results.

Look at top football coaches. They often have their best athlete on the bench waiting for a chance to replace a proven winner. The starter is playing because he has demonstrated results. He has proven he can win, even though he may be slower, lighter, and less agile than his teammate on the bench. What is valued more than his skills is his probability of winning.

What you have produced in the recent past is what gets noticed most. That's because future performance or results are best predicted by past performance or results. What counts are the results your stakeholders have seen and can predict, based on their understanding of your recent results.

It's vital for each of your stakeholders to understand your results and be able to relate them to their organizational or professional needs. It is up to you to make sure this happens, and your empathetic skills will help you here. As you do so, you will become more attractive to the influential people who create career options for you.

The first responsibility is yours: create results. The second responsibility is also yours: make sure your stakeholders know what you have created and are able to envision those results in bigger and more lucrative situations.

Before you know it, you will have taken a giant step toward maximizing your power to produce results. And those results will make you more valuable to your current and prospective bosses. As that happens, your career equity and professional freedom skyrocket—all because you used your skills to create results that turned into power.

3. Enhancing Your Skills

The third key is skills—relevant, current and constantly developing. Skills are what we generally acquire in school or through other investments of time and money in our professional development.

Your interpersonal skills, your time-management skills, leadership skills, computer skills, and even linguistic skills can count heavily toward maximizing your career options.

Personal Coach

1. Get to know each of your stakeholders well enough to discover how you might be able to give something of value to each of them. It could be a clipping from a magazine, an introduction, a kind word during a time of personal loss, attending (provided you are invited) life's punctuation mark events such as weddings, birthday parties, and family funerals, and helping at difficult times.

2. Target doing one thing at least every quarter to make all of your stakeholders' lives better—to help them get more of what they want professionally or personally.

3. Explore joining groups of successful managers, executives, or entrepreneurs who are already increasing their connections. Look for networking groups that have evolved into well-connected communities of professionals focused on helping each other succeed.

4. Join a group of well-connected leaders in your community, your church, your profession, or your company by becoming a volunteer. Then become a committee chair, the head of a fundraising effort, or a leader of something that stretches you and is fun. The group could

be The United Way, your chamber of commerce, or your credit union board.

5. Contact the head of your chamber of commerce, the local newspaper's top business editor, or a business school dean. Ask which connection-building (as opposed to contact-creating) group in your community would best fit your needs. Join one, and consistently give value to each member. You will feel good when you help them. This feeling will help you give even more.

6. Assess your strengths by scheduling time to write down a list of your strong connections, your most important stakeholders (and the opinions they may have of you based on your ability to produce results), and your skills.

7. Think smart. Determine how you could improve in each of the three key areas, focusing first on the most important—people power, then results, then skills.

8. Set specific goals to make the improvements in each of the three areas for each of the next four quarters.

9. Create accountability by sharing your goals with someone you respect and who will hold you accountable for follow-through. Set up quarterly progress and planning sessions with them.

CHAPTER 8

Political Power:
Get It or Lose It

Getting political power and using it effectively is usually a crucial skill ingredient in successful careers. Yet the subject of political power—how to get it and how to use it effectively for the betterment of your career, your department, and your company—is almost never taught.

His resentment of corporate America had been increasing for years because he didn't understand power. He still didn't understand when he was thirty-five years old, and that summer he chose not to be part of corporate America ever again.

We in the media lost a very special person who cared deeply about his fellow employees and about the First Amendment. The teaching profession gained a committed eighth-grade English teacher whose distrust of those who run this country's businesses was deeply embedded in his mind and emotions.

Now, twelve years later, he has a better understanding of the reasons for the decisions and situations that fueled his resentment—promotions, assignments, and relationships he had not been able to understand when they took place. He understands now and no longer holds his bias against power and those who have it.

He has grown up, perhaps too late for his dream career in newspaper journalism to come true. As he reminded me last week, "This stuff about political power should be taught in every Management 101 course. That way, more young people would have the training to recognize opportunities for acquiring and using power as they occur in their careers, communities, and churches."

My friend is wiser now. I hope others will be too after reading this chapter.

I have yet to see a management development course or a career-planning program aimed at sharpening the students' skills in this crucial area of professional performance. Listen to what Peter, the human resources manager at the local newspaper, has to say on this subject:

"I invest part of each week in acquiring or using my political power. It's the only way to get things done."

If you want to get things done better, sooner, and easier, do what champions do: get political power and use it. It's a key career competency.

Summarized below are eight political power tools used by successful careerists to get what they want. Before you put any of them in play, remember that like any tool used unwisely or incompetently, it can hurt you more than it helps you. So learn how (and when) to use each tool before attempting to build your career with it. This is an area where a professional coach who understands organizations can help you see and avoid pitfalls before they arise and advise you how to manage those that do.

Eight Political Power Tools Used in Successful Careers

1. Know where power is and where it is emerging, or have a mentor who knows.
2. Insert yourself into the informal and formal flows of information.
3. Be trusted.
4. Surround yourself with the trappings of power.
5. Compliment others in public.
6. Be entrepreneurial with your power.
7. Remember—everything counts.
8. Have a political power-building plan and coach.

Use your political power tools only after you have covered basics such as having a life purpose, a career plan, and making sure your boss is happy with your performance. Then launch your career to a new level by leveraging the might of your political power tools. Let's address each of these eight tools.

1. Know where power is and where it is emerging, or have a mentor who knows.

Knowing where the power lies, or having a mentor who can and will tell you where it exists, is the first step in using your political power tools.

During your first ninety days on a new job, make a determined effort to assess who has political power and who doesn't. Strive to perform this vital task as accurately as you can. Consider the idea of bell-cows. The leaders of a herd of cattle—or of any group of people— are called bell-cows. Top careerists figure out who the bell-cows are in their organizations, their industries, and their communities. They know how to focus their energy on influencing the people others follow, as a way to optimize their own career options and success.

Usually, your boss has enough political power to influence your career success to a substantial degree; so does his boss, and probably the boss the next level up.

However, determining where the power lies is rarely as simple as merely looking at the organizational chart. In very few organizations is real power actually exercised strictly along the lines given on the official chart.

Common sense tells us this truth: a powerful person who cares about you influences your career more than powerless people will. This is why you want to know quickly who the influencers are, and what expectations they have of you. What's your next step? Meet or exceed each influencer's expectations, and do it every time.

In most cases, political power regroups in different patterns for different decisions and purposes. Quite often, new channels of political power suddenly emerge to meet new challenges. Be alert for new challenges your company may find itself facing, because these pose great opportunities.

I have seen Bob, the human resources manager of our town's major bank group, scuttle a colleague's career by skillfully highlighting Pat's mistakes to top management. "I never thought we should have hired him in the first place," Bob said.

Simultaneously, I watched Joan (the bank president's daughter-in-law) and "only" a branch manager's assistant in the same banking group, champion another friend's career success for over ten years.

"Why?" I asked.

"From the first, I liked the way he treated people. So I thought he'd make a good executive some day," she told me.

We have all seen the CFO's standard response when he or she wants to restrict someone's success: "It's not in the budget." But when a friend's project is under consideration, a miracle happens. The same CFO somehow finds money to support it.

2. Insert yourself into the informal and formal flows of information.

Information is power. Inserting yourself into its formal and informal flows is a sure way to increase your political power. The switchboard operator (back in the days before computers took over this function) at our newspaper knew who was being recruited by competitors and who was having problems at home. She even knew which advertisers were very happy, and which ones seemed frustrated with a particular salesperson. The information she had was critical to the success of many careers.

I suspect the keepers of your company's informal information flow help someone's career every day and therefore, intentionally or not, hamper the careers of others. This process is virtually impossible to control by managerial edict, nor can you force it. The keepers have to want to help your career. Make sure they do.

Formal information comes from budgets, databases, and reports. Control formal information to build your power. I have seen chief financial officers, information technology directors, and vice presidents for human resources accumulate more power than their bosses by maximizing the usable information they glean from their access to these.

Gary was the quality control technician. Each month his reports made heroes or bums of the ten production supervisors. Sam, one of the ten, was a friend of Gary's. Quite naturally, Gary and Sam fell into a routine of discussing the reports over lunch before they were delivered to the superintendent.

Sam, you won't be surprised to learn, was always the best prepared to discuss quality performance issues during the plant superintendent's meetings. Access to these reports before his peers saw them was helpful to Sam's success with that company.

3. Be trusted.

To accumulate a considerable amount of political power, you must be trusted by the organization's most powerful people, or at least by those who have power over your career success.

To be trusted by the powerful people, you'll want to be highly regarded for your attitudes, values, and ethics as they are understood by important people.

Also essential to being trusted are your behaviors vs. what you say you'll do. In other words, can you be trusted to behave the way you say you will? Will you follow through? Can you follow through, given the power of your position?

A third ingredient to being trusted is the company you keep. As my mother said when I was growing up,

"You are known by the people you hang out with. If I trust them, I feel I can trust you."

4. Surround yourself with trappings of power.

Displaying a picture of you and the president at last year's company picnic, or having your college diploma on the wall when everyone knows the CEO graduated from the same school are ways to surround yourself with the trappings of power.

Having lunch with the boss's son at the town's most popular restaurant, or wearing a shirt with the top country club's logo are other frequently seen examples of surrounding yourself with power trappings. The theme is associating yourself with power.

5. Compliment others in public.

Giving sincere compliments at the annual shareholder's meeting, or at your weekly staff meeting, conveys political power.

After all, if you give accolades—and therefore power—to someone else, you must have had it in order to give it.

But be wary here. Even though complimenting in public is one of the easiest techniques for creating political power, it can also be one of the riskiest if it appears to be insincere.

6. Be entrepreneurial with your power.

Being entrepreneurial with your political power, through risk-taking, is a good way to multiply it. Hoarding your political power will probably cause it to atrophy.

Wisely risk your political power by getting involved in big projects or working in high-flying divisions. Take on a particularly difficult community volunteer assignment, like chairing your company's United Way campaign. This can put your name and career on senior management's radar screen, especially when the results are seen positively.

7. Remember: Everything Counts.

As mentioned in other chapters, everything you do has the potential to impact your career and political power. What occupies your mind in odd moments at work? Last night's TV sitcom instead of next quarter's marketing plan? Are you reading material that enhances your power base?

Developing strong empathy skills will help you know what will positively impress one person and turn off another—so work at developing your ability to attune to others.

Make your decisions, from the smallest to the largest, based on this fact of life: everything counts!

8. Have a political power—building plan and coach.

Keeping track of everything can be overwhelming, which is why many people with successful careers have coaches to help them keep focused on getting the right results, strengthening their empathetic leadership skills, and perfecting their political power tools. You can, too.

By doing these eight things well, you will have more resources, more freedom to take risks—and therefore more opportunities to win big—and you'll be better able to attract the best bosses and the best jobs. You'll have more power to get what you want for your department, your company, and yourself.

Today is the day to start sharpening your political power tools.

Personal Coach

1. Find a political power mentor or coach, and develop a plan to be more powerful each year.

2. Decide how you will insert yourself into the flow of information.

3. Know who has political power, and who will probably have political power next year. Then get them to want to help you by helping them.

4. Identify one way you can exhibit a trapping of power.

5. Be on the lookout for opportunities to sincerely compliment others for specific reasons.

6. Know what the most powerful people in your organization expect of you, and then meet those expectations better than those with whom you are compared.

A Closing Thought: Sing Your Song

My song is:

> Row, Row, Row Your Boat
> Gently Down the Stream
> Merrily, Merrily, Merrily, Merrily
> Life Is But a Dream

This little song reminds me to row my boat. Not someone else's boat. Mine. At the same time, it reminds me to not let others row my boat. After all, it's my boat to row, with both arms, in balance, or I risk going around in circles!

It also reminds me to be gentle with life. Champions usually make it look effortless because they have become so good at what they do through relaxed concentration and focus.

Third, it reminds me I have an option each day to be merry or sad, to see opportunities or problems, to see the good in others or the bad. It is my choice how I experience each day.

Last, it reminds me that my life is but my dream's coming true. I am the only one who can give me my dream. I am the only one among the world's billions who can make my dream come true.

My wish for you is that you give yourself a song. I hope it is a song you find in your heart, and that it helps you make your career dream come true. Write a life plan that is supported by your written career plan. Be passionate about your work and keep a song in your heart. By doing so, you can attract as many resources and supporters as you need.

Suggested Readings

Bergquist, William, Greenberg, Elinor and Klaum, Alan (1993). *In Our Fifties*. Jossey-Bass Publishers.

Boldt, Laurence (1993). *Zen and the Art of Making a Living*. Penguin Books.

Bridges, William (1980). *Transitions*. Perseus Books.

Buckingham, Marcus and Coffman, Curt (1999). *First, Break All the Rules*. Simon & Schuster.

Buckingham, Marcus (2001). *Now, Discover Your Strengths* (abridged audio). Free Press.

Canfield, Jack (2000). *The Power of Focus*. Health Communications.

Cashman, Kevin (1999). *Leadership From The Inside Out: Becoming a Leader for Life*. Executive Excellence Publishing (note: the audio version is acceptable).

Coffman, Curt and Gonzalez-Molina, Gabriel (2002). *Follow This Path*. Warner Books.

Covey, Stephen (1994). *First Things First*. Simon & Schuster.

Covey, Stephen (1989). *The Seven Habits of Highly Effective People*. Simon & Schuster.

Csikszentmihalyi, Mihaly (1990). *Flow*. Harper & Row.

Drucker, Peter (1954). *The Practice of Management*. HarperCollins Publishers, Inc.

Epictetus (1994). *The Art of Living*. HarperCollins Publishers, Inc.

Frankl, Victor (2000). *Mans Search for Meaning*. Beacon Press.

Gladwell, Malcolm (2000). *The Tipping Point! How Little Things Can Make a Big Difference*. Little Brown & Company.

Goldsmith, Marshall, Lyons, Laurence, and Freas, Alyssa (2000).*Coaching for Leadership*. Jossey-Bass Publishers.

Goleman, Daniel (1995). *Emotional Intelligence*. Bantam Books.

Goleman, Daniel (1998). *Working with Emotional Intelligence* (note: the audio version is acceptable). Bantam Books.

Goleman, Daniel (2002). *Primal Leadership*. Harvard Business School Publishing.

Hudson, Frederic (1999). *The Adult Years*. Jossey-Bass Publishing.

Jampolsky, Gerald (1979). *Love is Letting Go of Fear*. Celestial Arts.

Johnson, Spencer (1998). *Who Moved My Cheese?* Putnam Publishing Group.

Jones, Laurie (1996). *The Path*. Henry Holt Co.

Katzenbach, Jon (2000). *Peak Performance*. Harvard Business School Publishing.

Keirsey, David (1998). *Please Understand Me II*. Prometheus Nemesis Book Co.

Korda, Michael (1975). *Power! How to Get It, How to Use It*. Random House, Inc.

Kouzes, James and Posner, Barry (2003). *Encouraging the Heart*. John Wiley & Sons, Inc.

Kouzes, James and Posner,Barry (2002). *The Leadership Challenge*. Third Edition. Jossey-Bass.

Leider, Richard and Shapiro, David (1996). *Repacking Your Bags*. MJF Books.

Leonard, George (1992). *Mastery*. Blume Publishing.

Maister, David (2000). *True Professionalism*. Touchstone Books.

Maslow, Abraham (1998). *Maslow on Management*. John Wiley & Sons.

McGraw, Phillip (2000). *Relationship Rescue*. Hyperion.

McNally, David and Speak, Karl D. (2002). *Be Your Own Brand*. Berrett-Koehler Publishers, Inc.

Nerburn, Kent (2002). *Simple Truths*. Barnes & Noble Books.

Niven, David (2000). *The 100 Simple Secrets of Happy People*. HarperCollins Publisher, Inc.

O'Neil, John (1994). *The Paradox of Success*. J.P. Tarcher.

Peck, Scott (1993). *The Road Less Traveled*. Simon and Schuster, Inc.

Prager, Dennis (1998). *Happiness is a Serious Problem*. HarperCollins Publisher, Inc.

Ruiz, Don Miguel (1997). *The Four Agreements*. Amber-Allen Publishing.

Sanders, Tim (2002). *Love is the Killer APP.* Crown Publishing Group.

Schwartz, Tony (1995). *What Really Matters*. Bantam.

Seligman, Martin (2002). *Authentic Happiness*. Simon & Schuster.

Seligman, Martin (1998). *Learned Optimism: How to Change Your Mind and Your Life.* Simon & Schuster.

Senn, Larry (1999). *The Secrets of a Winning Culture.* The Leadership Press.

Thrall, Bill (1999). *The Ascent of a Leader.* Jossey-Bass.

Wilkinson, Bruce (2000). *The Prayer of Jabez.* Multnomah Publishers, Inc.

Zander, Rosamund Stone and Zander, Benjamin (2000). *The Art of Possibility.* Harvard Business School Publishing.

Order Form

Mail to: Vance Caesar Group
3020 Old Ranch Parkway, Third Floor
Seal Beach, CA 90740

Name _____

Title _____

Address _____

City _____

State/Zip _____

Phone (___)_____   Fax (___)_____

QUANTITY	TITLE	UNIT PRICE	AMOUNT

Subtotal	_____
S&H, $3.50 for 1 book, $4.50 for 2, $5.50 for 3	_____
Sales Tax	_____
California Residents add 7.75 % Sales Tax	_____
Total	_____

Please make check or money order payable to:
The Vance Caesar Group